Who Is God?

Leading Children to God by Asking Questions

Jane Reed

WestBow Press books may be ordered through booksellers or by contacting:

WestBow Press
A Division of Thomas Nelson & Zondervan
1663 Liberty Drive
Bloomington, IN 47403
www.westbowpress.com
844.714.3454

ISBN: 978-1-6642-1183-4 (sc)
ISBN: 978-1-6642-1185-8 (hc)
ISBN: 978-1-6642-1184-1 (e)

Library of Congress Control Number: 2020922101

Print information available on the last page.

WestBow Press rev. date: 11/30/2020

WestBow
PRESS®
A DIVISION OF THOMAS NELSON
& ZONDERVAN

This Book is a special gift for

_____

Given with love by

_____

Date: _____

An Important Preview Invitation for Parents, Grandparents, Teachers, and "Reading Buddies"

Please read this insightful letter first to discover an effective approach for inter-active learning.

Would you like a dynamic way to introduce the children you love to God?

This book is built on questions! Amazingly, Inquiry-Based Learning is the most powerful way to lead and teach effectively. Why? Inquiry is the way God naturally created us to learn from birth. Every time we hear, see, or touch we initiate an inquiry. Current research has shown that inquiry stimulates greater interest than telling. When we tell children what to do and what to believe, they quickly lose interest and forget our wonderful words of loving wisdom. However, when we ask questions, we engage their minds and hearts and ignite a desire to learn and understand. This is called curiosity, the initiator of a growth mindset!

Children are born curious and begin life searching for meaning. Because children are created in God's image, they have a need and a longing to reach out to know God long before they can speak or walk. As unique individuals, they want to develop their own relationship with the One who created them. As parents and leaders, we must remember that the condition of each child's heart will determine the values by which he or she will live.

I regret that when I was a young mother, I assumed my children would come to know God because I did. So, I believed they would learn to pray, read their Bibles, and develop a relationship with God just because I set the example. However, I often prayed and read my Bible in private. When we prayed as a family, Mom or Dad often did all the communicating. Sadly, religion seemed more of a thing their parents and others "did," than a way of living they could embrace in their own way. I somehow forgot that God wants to have a personal relationship with each of them, not just a borrowed version of mine. God wants them to hear Him when He calls them by name. Many times, religion may have seemed like just a set of restrictive rules they should obey, rather than a meaningful relationship with a heavenly Father who actually loves them. Now I wonder if this is because I supplied and owned all the answers about faith, and never invited my children to ask their own questions about God.

This book is written to read to your children from birth, as you rock them and hold them close to your heart. Word by word, and moment by moment, you will be developing an environment that acknowledges and worships God. Don't worry that they may not understand all the words at this stage of life. Reading will develop a vocabulary that includes and prioritizes learning about God. You will be inviting and allowing God to nurture your child's beautiful heart! Can you imagine the impact that will have?

<u>Children love repetition</u>, so continue reading this book often as your children become toddlers. If it seems too long, just read a portion each day. To deepen and enrich learning you can include some of the interactive questions, where your children ask you to share personal experiences and insights. When your children have the book memorized, or develop reading skills, allow them to read the book to you. Speaking the words themselves will lead them to remember the words and use them in a personal way to guide their lives. Encourage your children to <u>ask their own questions.</u> When children begin to ask their own questions, it is a sign that they are excited, interested and eager to learn. It is also the beginning of what we call, "Flipped Communication" ™. (Check out our next book to learn more!) Our ultimate objective is to inspire every child to ask God questions, too!

My hope is that you will grow together in your love for the Lord, while establishing worship as a valuable part of your home.

May you cherish your moments together!

Hugs,
Jane

Who Is God?

Who is God? Have you ever heard grown-ups talk about God and wondered, "**Who** are they talking about?" God is the One who created the world we live in. He made Mom, Dad, your Family, and He made YOU!

Who is God? The One who loved you first. He is the One who will always love you!

Would you like to learn something awesome?

Even though God created everything in the world (even things we can't see)

He still cherishes you. You are precious to Him!

Who is God? The One who will always love you!

Do you know that God designed you with His own hands and imagination? He put the stars in your eyes, the smile on your face, and the love in your heart!

♥   Can you share your beautiful smile and starry eyes with the person reading this book?

I imagine it will bring you a big warm hug! How about a smile for God? He will cherish your smile like a bright ray of sunshine!

Who is God? The One who will always love you!

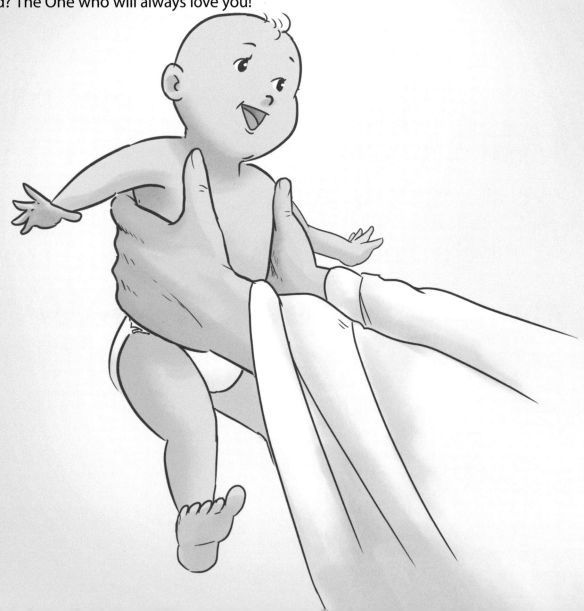

Who are you? Are you a fluffy kitten? Are you a soft and cuddly blanket? Are you a cozy rocking chair? No! You are a child of God! Wow! What could be more amazing than that?

Who is God? The One who will always love you!

What does God do? He provides everything you see in the world and always takes special care of His Creation: sunshine, rain, wind, trees, bluebirds, flowers, snowflakes, grass, bugs.

Being curious helps you get to know God and makes all learning exciting!

Can you curiously look around and notice more things God created? **What** did you find? Anything you can name has God's fingerprint on it! (Even sand and rocks!)

What does God do? He always loves you!

Can you see the fingerprint on the rock? **How** many more can you find?

Where is God? Everywhere! God is in your house, the sky, the air, the clouds and He is in your heart. Nothing can separate you from God! **Where** will God find you? Wherever you are!

Who is God? God is the One who will always love you anywhere and everywhere you go!

Why can't I see God? God is too big for a body! If God had a body, He would be limited! That means He could only be in one place at a time and only do one thing at a time. Even though He has an entire universe to care for, He wants to sit beside you and beside every other person, no matter where they are. God's presence is everywhere!

Why does God want to be with you? Because He is the One who will always love you!

What else do I need to know? Even though we can't see God, He is always near and has enormous power! He is there for you, everyone you know, and everyone you don't know. God has the power to touch your heart and make it beautiful!

Who is God? The source of all power, and the One who will always love you!

How can I see God's power?

Look around. God's power radiates in everything you see! He makes the wind blow the ocean waves and the sun come up every morning. He keeps the whole world running smoothly!

Why does God share His power? Because He cares for you and He is the One who will always love you!

Does God know how much we want to see Him? God knew people would feel more comforted if they could see Him. God has a Son. His name is Jesus. God sent Jesus into our world long ago, so people could see Him, touch Him, and hear His voice. Jesus came to show us how we should live. You will want to get to know Jesus. There are great stories about Him in God's word, the Bible. Jesus is proof that God exists!

♥   Would you like to ask your special reader to share some Bible stories about Jesus?

Who is Jesus? God's Son, who will always love you!

What did Jesus teach? Jesus taught us how to love God with all of our hearts! He also taught us to love everyone we meet. Jesus gives us the strength to do what is good and true and right. He came into the world so we would never be separated from His Father!

♥ How does your loving reader get strength from Jesus?

Why should you learn more about Jesus? Because He and His Father will always love you!

How can I tell Jesus I love Him? You can talk with Jesus and God at the same time! They would love to have a conversation with you. That's called prayer. You can talk to them anytime. They are always listening and love to hear your voice. Tell them you love them. That will make their hearts jump for joy!

Who is God? **Who** is Jesus? The Father and Son who will always love you!

Can you think of some things you would like to say to God? He would love to have you ask Him questions. Questions start with words you are hearing in this book, "who," "what," "when," "where," "why," and "how." Ask God anything. God knows all the secrets of the universe!

♥ Not sure how to ask God a question? Your special person who is reading to you would love to help you learn.

Who is God? The One who loves to hear your questions and will always love you!

How can I hear God? Just be calm and quiet. Then wait and listen for His answers. Another way to hear God is to read the Bible. You will always be amazed by what you learn!

- ♥ This is a great time to ask your loving reader to help you find some answers to your questions in the Bible.

Who is God? The One who loves to speak with you because He will always love you!

Why don't we take a minute to talk about more ways to show God you love him? You can show your love by being kind to everyone you meet. Can you think of nice things to say to others? When can you share your toys? How can you listen when someone else speaks? Do you know someone who needs a hug? When we care for others, we are sharing God's love!

Who is God? The One whose warm heart will always love you!

What else makes God happy? Another way to show God how much you love Him is to be grateful. When we say "Thank-you" to God, He feels happy. It will make you feel happy, too! What things can you thank God for? When we are grateful, our hearts are in tune with God's heart!

♥   What makes your special reader grateful?

Why should we thank God for His blessings? That's how you show God that <u>you</u> will always love Him!

What would make God sad? It breaks God's heart when we forget about Him. So, look for Him and speak with Him often. His heart aches when we disobey our parents. Oh, how His heart hurts when we say bad things or bully other children. How do you think God feels when we forget to share or take something that does not belong to us?

These things hurt all of us. Our hearts will feel sad and broken. That's when we need Jesus to set things right!

How does Jesus make things right? He will wash away your mistakes, because He is the One who will always love you!

What should I do when I have hurt God with my words or actions? Tell Him you are sorry. When you ask for forgiveness, God will heal your broken heart. He will always give you another chance!

Who is God? The One who forgives you and heals your heart, because He will always love you!

How can God help me make better choices? You can give God a chance to help you by praying before you speak or act. You will always be on the right path when you choose to act in a way that would delight Jesus. Most of all, love God more than anything else.

Remember, God is always close to you, even when you make mistakes. He wants to hear you sing to Him as He holds you tenderly in His arms!

♥ When has the person reading to you felt hugged by God?

Who is God? He is the One who will always love you!

When can I reach out to God? Anytime and all the time! God calls your name and asks you to run to Him. He's inviting you to look for Him, and He can't wait for the precious moment when you will find Him! **When** does God welcome you? ALWAYS!

Who is God? The One who will always love you!

Am I important to God? You sure are! He designed you to be just the way you are, a unique design of endless possibilities! You are so important to God that He has big plans for you to make a positive difference in the world! He can use you right now, right where you are.

Can you imagine what those plans might be?

God can!

Who is God? The One who will always love you!

No matter what!

Dear Tender-Hearted Child,

When the love of God lives in your heart, He will make you fine and noble, great and good. Your life will glorify God and you will be a blessing to others!

Who is God?

The One who will always love you!

Printed in the United States
By Bookmasters